What's for lunch?

This edition 2003

Franklin Watts
96 Leonard Street
London
EC2A 4XD

Franklin Watts Australia
45-51 Huntley Street
Alexandria
NSW 2015

Editor: Samantha Armstrong
Series Designer: Kirstie Billingham
Designer: Jason Anscomb
Consultant: British Egg Information Service
Reading Consultant: Prue Goodwin, Reading and Language
Information Centre, Reading

A CIP catalogue record for this book is available from the British Library
Dewey Decimal Classification Number 641.3

ISBN: 0 7496 4938 0

Printed in Hong Kong, China

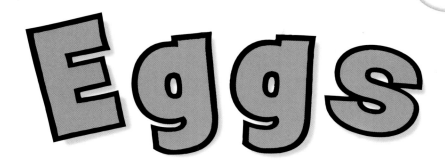

What's for lunch?

Eggs

Claire Llewellyn

W
FRANKLIN WATTS
LONDON • SYDNEY

Today we are having eggs for lunch.
Eggs contain **protein, vitamins** and
minerals. They help us to grow
and stay healthy.

5

We eat eggs laid by hens, ducks or geese.
All these birds are farmyard birds.
Another name for them is **poultry.**
They are usually kept on poultry farms.

Most of the eggs we eat are hens' eggs.
Sometimes eggs have been **fertilized**
and **hatch** into baby chicks.
But the eggs we eat have not been fertilized.
They could never hatch into chicks.

Hens' eggs can have white,
brown or speckled shells.
It depends on the **breed** of hen.

On poultry farms hens lay eggs
all the year round.
The farmer removes the eggs each day.

There are different kinds of poultry farms.
On **free-range** farms, hens wander outside.
They peck about looking for insects,
worms, roots and leaves.
Free-range hens sleep in a henhouse.
The eggs are collected from the henhouse
and taken to the packing room.

Battery farms are another kind of poultry farm.
The hens are kept inside cages,
with four or five hens in each cage.
The birds are given food and water
every few hours.
Their eggs are taken on a **conveyor belt**
to the packing room.

In the packing room,
the eggs are checked for cracks or faults.
The egg checkers use a special light
to see inside the eggs,
and check that they are good to eat.
This is called **candling.**

The good eggs are sorted into different sizes
and packed into boxes.
The boxes are labelled to show
where and when the eggs were laid
and when they should be eaten.
Some shops like their eggs to be stamped
so that customers can see
if they are fresh enough to use.

21

The eggs are then delivered to markets, shops and supermarkets.
Eggs are usually sold in groups of twelve.
Twelve eggs are known as a **dozen**.
Six eggs are known as half a dozen.

Any eggs that are cracked or are an odd shape
are sold to food manufacturers.
At the factory, the eggs are broken
and specially treated to keep them fresh.
This is called **pasteurization.**